STOI

MW00379486

If you are the purchaser of this book, go to:

www.thegoodkarmabook.com/register

Enter your name and click "Generate Book ID" and you will be assigned a unique ID number.

Write your assigned ID number on the inside FRONT COVER
(largely and clearly!)

Once you have written your number on the inside front cover, you can write it here and tear out this page to keep for your records:

_____

Thank you for purchasing and spreading
THE GOOD KARMA

Congratulations on finding The Good Karma Book!

You were destined to pass on The Good Karma.

1. Do a good deed for this World. It can be a grand gesture or simply a smile, holding the door or picking up a piece of trash. The sky is the limit.

2. Sign this logbook and record the Good Karma you created. You can do so anonymously if you wish!

3. (Optional) Go to www.thegoodkarmabook.com and help log this book's Good Karma travels!
    - Click on "I Found The Good Karma Book!", enter the number written on the inside front cover of this book and record your location and Good Karma.

4. Keep it going. Leave this book somewhere for another to find The Good Karma.

Other Fun...

Visit The Good Karma Book on Facebook to post photos, etc of your finds!

www.facebook.com/thegoodkarmabook/

Date	Name	Where Found?	City/State/ Country	Good Karma Spread

Help log this book's travels at www.thegoodkarmabook.com

You will never
regret being kind.

Date	Name	Where Found?	City/State/Country	Good Karma Spread

Help log this book's travels at www.thegoodkarmabook.com

Everything

You Do

Comes Back

to You

Date	Name	Where Found?	City/State/ Country	Good Karma Spread

Help log this book's travels at www.thegoodkarmabook.com

"A hero is a man,

that does what he can."

- Romain Rolland

Date	Name	Where Found?	City/State/ Country	Good Karma Spread

Help log this book's travels at www.thegoodkarmabook.com

"To be good, and do good, is the whole duty of man comprised in a few words."

- Abigail Adams

Date	Name	Where Found?	City/State/Country	Good Karma Spread

Help log this book's travels at www.thegoodkarmabook.com

"Happiness never

decreases

by being

shared."

- Gautama Buddha

Date	Name	Where Found?	City/State/Country	Good Karma Spread

Help log this book's travels at www.thegoodkarmabook.com

"The creation of a thousand forests is in one acorn."

- Ralph Waldo Emerson

Date	Name	Where Found?	City/State/ Country	Good Karma Spread

Help log this book's travels at www.thegoodkarmabook.com

"Try and fail,

but don't fail

to try."

- John Quincy Adams

Date	Name	Where Found?	City/State/ Country	Good Karma Spread

Help log this book's travels at www.thegoodkarmabook.com

"The beginning is the most important part of the work..."

- Plato

Date	Name	Where Found?	City/State/ Country	Good Karma Spread

Help log this book's travels at www.thegoodkarmabook.com

"As the purse is emptied, the heart is filled."

- Victor Hugo

Date	Name	Where Found?	City/State/ Country	Good Karma Spread

Help log this book's travels at www.thegoodkarmabook.com

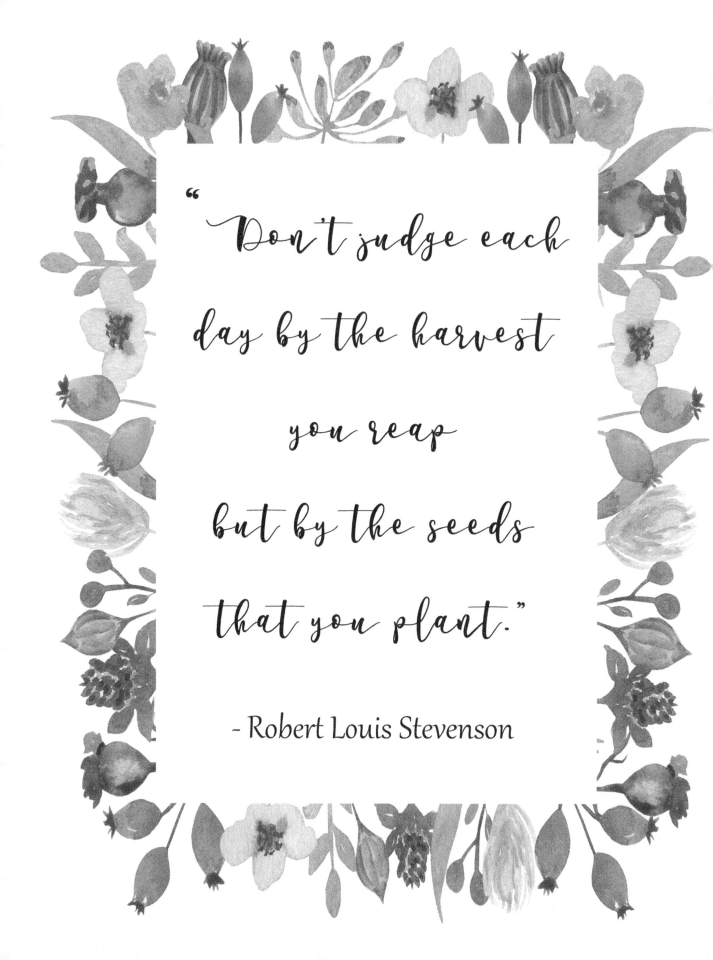

"Don't judge each day by the harvest you reap but by the seeds that you plant."

- Robert Louis Stevenson

Date	Name	Where Found?	City/State/ Country	Good Karma Spread

Help log this book's travels at www.thegoodkarmabook.com

"Happiness is when what you think, what you say, and what you do are in harmony."

- Mahatma Gandhi

Date	Name	Where Found?	City/State/Country	Good Karma Spread

Help log this book's travels at www.thegoodkarmabook.com

I believe compassion to be one of the few things we can practice that will bring immediate and long-term happiness to our lives.

- Dalai Lama

Date	Name	Where Found?	City/State/ Country	Good Karma Spread

Help log this book's travels at www.thegoodkarmabook.com

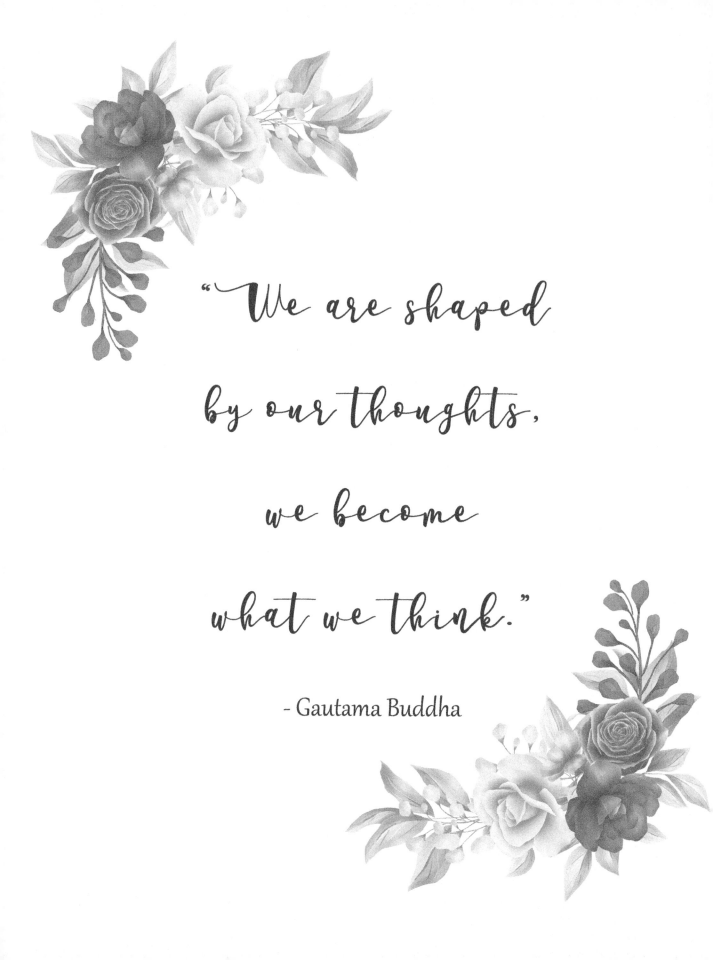

"We are shaped by our thoughts, we become what we think."

- Gautama Buddha

Date	Name	Where Found?	City/State/Country	Good Karma Spread

Help log this book's travels at www.thegoodkarmabook.com

"Always stand on
principle,
even if you stand
alone."

- John Adams

Date	Name	Where Found?	City/State/ Country	Good Karma Spread

Help log this book's travels at www.thegoodkarmabook.com

"Well done is better than well said."

- Benjamin Franklin

Date	Name	Where Found?	City/State/Country	Good Karma Spread

Help log this book's travels at www.thegoodkarmabook.com

"Happiness is the only good.
The time to be happy is now.
The place to be happy is here.
The way to be happy is
to make others so."

- Robert Ingersoll

Date	Name	Where Found?	City/State/ Country	Good Karma Spread

Help log this book's travels at www.thegoodkarmabook.com

"Positive anything
is better than
negative nothing"

- Elbert Hubbard

Date	Name	Where Found?	City/State/Country	Good Karma Spread

"Love inspires,

illuminates,

designates,

and leads the way."

- Mary Baker Eddy

Date	Name	Where Found?	City/State/Country	Good Karma Spread

Help log this book's travels at www.thegoodkarmabook.com

"The Best Way to Predict the Future, is to Create it."

- Abraham Lincoln

Date	Name	Where Found?	City/State/ Country	Good Karma Spread

"If your actions inspire others to dream more, do more and become more, you are a leader."

-John Quincy Adams

Date	Name	Where Found?	City/State/ Country	Good Karma Spread

"A person often meets his destiny on the road he took to avoid it."

- Jean de La Fontaine

Date	Name	Where Found?	City/State/ Country	Good Karma Spread

"He who cannot give anything away cannot feel anything either."

- Friedrich Nietzsche

Date	Name	Where Found?	City/State/ Country	Good Karma Spread

"A superior man is modest in his speech, but exceeds in his actions."

- Confucius

Date	Name	Where Found?	City/State/ Country	Good Karma Spread

Help log this book's travels at www.thegoodkarmabook.com

"Life is ten percent what happens to you, and ninety percent how you respond to it."

- Lou Holtz

Date	Name	Where Found?	City/State/ Country	Good Karma Spread

Help log this book's travels at www.thegoodkarmabook.com

"Knowing is not enough;

we must apply.

Willing is not enough;

we must do."

- Johann Wolfgang von Goethe

Date	Name	Where Found?	City/State/ Country	Good Karma Spread

"Beware of missing chances,

otherwise it may

be altogether

too late some day."

- Franz Liszt

Date	Name	Where Found?	City/State/ Country	Good Karma Spread

Help log this book's travels at www.thegoodkarmabook.com

"The value of an idea lies in the using of it."

- Thomas Edison

Date	Name	Where Found?	City/State/ Country	Good Karma Spread

Help log this book's travels at www.thegoodkarmabook.com

"One of the first signs of a spirit-filled life is enthusiasm."

- A.B. Simpson

Date	Name	Where Found?	City/State/ Country	Good Karma Spread

Help log this book's travels at www.thegoodkarmabook.com

"Whatever

you are,

be a good one."

- Abraham Lincoln

Date	Name	Where Found?	City/State/Country	Good Karma Spread

Help log this book's travels at www.thegoodkarmabook.com

"The only wealth
which you keep forever,
is the wealth,
you have given away."

-Marcus Aurelius

Made in the USA
Monee, IL
17 January 2021

55608568R00037